HANDLING INFIDELITY

WHAT TO DO WHEN YOUR PARTNER CHEATS YOU

Third Edition: June 2022

Jiten Bhatt asserts the moral right to be identified as the author of this book.

Freebies for you

Freebies for you on the last page of this book.

Dedicated to all those who are suffering from Infidelity.

Don't worry, things will be okay.

<u>Remember, "This too shall pass..."</u>

Index

My Apology

While I have made the utmost efforts in rectifying all the grammatical errors in this book, yet you will find a few instances where there is scope for improvement. My native language is not English, and so despite my best efforts, I am pretty sure I would have missed out on something. So, I apologise for all such errors, and I humbly request you to focus on the central idea of the book. I hope you gain something valuable after reading this book, and this book provides you with value for your money. And yes, if you found this book of any value, do write a review, if possible, because it will help me a lot. I once again thank you for sparing your valuable time and money for selecting my book when there were several other choices. God bless you. Be happy and keep smiling.

1 Congratulations

Did you just realize that your partner is cheating on you? This giant heap of trouble might have poured into your life just now or maybe a few days ago or even a few months before, but trust me, it's not a pleasant situation to deal with. Let us first take a deep breath and relax because you will need a lot of patience to deal with this situation. You might have given your hundred percent to this relationship, despite that your partner is taking you on a bumpy ride in your life. Your heart must be filled with anger and pain. You might appear perfectly ok from outside to others but from inside, your stress levels could be enormously high. You might not feel like talking to anyone or going outside. You might be even crying inside you, if not outside. The entire world might seem like a dirty place to live in. But the thing you need to realize is this,

---

"You can either let circumstances choose your happiness or you can choose your happiness irrespective of your circumstances."

There is an Indian saying in the Hindi language that says,

"पुरे हे वो मर्द जो हर हल में खुस हे,

It means a person is complete if he is happy irrespective of his circumstances. If he receives wealth, then he is happy with the wealth, but if he goes broke, then he is still happy being broke.

This might sound like a textbook dialogue, and there is no sense of being happy when you are in such a traumatic situation where the love of your life is cheating on you. But life is full of difficulties and presently you are in a downstate of your life, where nothing is going the same way as you had expected. Though it sounds very harsh, the truth is that your relationship is failing. The sooner you accept it, the easier it will be to come out of this situation and have a positive solution. So first, take a deep, calm breath and relax for a while. Put your anger aside for a while and be in this moment with yourself.

First, tap yourself and congratulate yourself. This might sound crazy, but trust me, there are several reasons why you should celebrate this situation.

Accept that you are in this situation, so your life is going on, and you are realizing different facets of life. Remember, if there are no heartbeats then you are dead, so at this moment life is presenting you with its different facets and you should be happy about that. Don't curse your life for showing you this day, rather smile and adopt this moment. If you are a Hindi song lover, pause reading this book and listen to the song,

---

"Ae Zindagi gale laga le, humne bhi, tere har ek gam ko, gale se lagaya hai na!"

This is a popular Bollywood song, which is asking life to give a close hug as the singer has bravely hugged all the pain given by life. Alternately, how about listening to the song *"I will survive"* by Gloria Gaynor. Even before we address the topic of how to deal with a cheating partner, let's pause for a while and cheer up for some time.

Another big reason why you need to smile in this situation is that life is teaching you some very important lessons. I am not yet commenting on the modality of the situation like, is your cheating partner guilty or, he/she should be punished. All I am telling now is to look at things from a fresh perspective. It is but natural that you want sympathy because you are in deep trouble. But if you look at things from a wider perspective, by bringing you into this situation, life is trying to teach you a very important lesson. And if you can get to this point, then life is trying to point out something to you. God is very kind to everyone. Despite bringing you into this situation, God is still with you and wants you to understand an important lesson,

You might not be responsible for this situation. You might have given your hundred percent, but please understand that life is unfair many times.

A deer might think it has killed no one and throughout its life, it has only eaten grass. So, it is unfair for the lion to eat the deer. But as you know, lions don't eat grass and they must kill the deer to survive. It's part of the food cycle. Do you realize you are very close to the situation of the deer? So, break this mentality of fairness and unfairness and become strong in life. If a deer must survive, it cannot sit and cry, it has to become stronger and run faster than the lion. Likewise, you must get up and become strong, so that you are not eaten away by the lion. Remember the proverb,

And if any of the above points are still not convincing you, then think about this. According to research from a new study by YouGov, approximately one in five people surveyed admitted to cheating on their partner. One in five is a huge number! That means you are not alone in this world, who is facing this situation, there are many and most of them have successfully come out of this situation. So, you will come out too.

On that note, before reading further, let us just for a moment celebrate this situation. People often celebrate the happy times they spend with their partners. You celebrate your anniversary, your first date and other such happy moments you spent with your partner. Don't you? Then why not celebrate this painful moment arising because of your partner today? After all, life is not only about happy moments. It is about celebrating the tough times as well.

In the remaining chapters of this book, I will guide you through a step-by-step process on how you can come out of this situation. I don't guarantee a patch up with your partner, but I guarantee that by the end of this book you would be a better person, a stronger person, and a more practical person. So, keep reading. But before that please bring a big smile on your face. You look good when you smile. So, keep smiling.

"Use your smile to change the world,

Don't let the world change your smile!"

2 Confirm before you cry

A man calls up his home to speak to his wife. The maid picks up the phone and so the man asks,
"Connect me to my wife."

"I am sorry Sir, but she is with someone in the bedroom and has asked me not to disturb her", replies the maid.

On hearing this, the man becomes furious and says,
"I will offer you one million dollars if you shoot both of them."

The maid agrees, and soon the man hears three gunshots. The maid returns to the phone and says,
"Done, Sir. The man was trying to run away and so I had to shoot him the second time near the swimming pool."

The man says, "We don't have a swimming pool. Is this 554-4329???"

I hope this brings the much-awaited smile on your face. Jokes apart, but you too need to re-confirm whether you are really having a cheating partner or it's just an illusion to you. In modern times of Facebook and WhatsApp, sending messages with heart emojis or likes on photos is quite common among male and female friends. Every conversation of your partner with the opposite sex need not be an affair. It might be just a close friendship.

Hence, recall when and how did you realize that your partner was cheating on you? Have you confirmed about this through any other means? Are you sure about your conclusion? Many times, a small misunderstanding can create a havoc in a married life. Hence, before we learn to swim in the ocean of infidelity, let us be doubly sure whether we are sinking in this ocean. Also, at this point let us briefly understand the different types of Infidelity.

Types of Infidelity

It is important to understand that infidelity has existed ever since marriage was invented. But in today's scenario, it is even more difficult to define infidelity as its definition keeps on expanding. Earlier we used to have the belief that **"we marry until death does us apart"**. But today in this modern society where divorce is a common thing, **"we marry until love dies"**.

There are multiple types of infidelity. Most of the time people believe it is about sex, but it is not just sex, there are many forms of infidelity. According to Kimberly Holmes, the CEO of Marriage Helper, which is one of the largest organizations that works with love affairs on a day-to-day basis. According to the research, most types of infidelity stem from three main biological needs that people have in a relationship. These three needs are sexual, physical and emotional.

The first form of infidelity is sexual infidelity, where it's just all about sex. Your partner might just be indulging in a casual sexual encounter, one-night stand, or just a long-term physical-only relationship. The major reason for this type of infidelity is the desire for sex, which can be because of multiple reasons such as unsatisfactory sex-life among partners, higher sex-drive and urges among individuals, addictions to porn, infatuations or even fetish desires among individuals. If your partner is having a casual encounter or one-night stand, then for you, it might be relatively easy to deal with, since he/she might have strong emotional feelings for you. Many times, people get distracted because of multiple reasons and are also ashamed and feel guilty later.

The second type of infidelity is emotional infidelity. This infidelity is more about the emotional and relational connection between two people rather than the physical connection. This type of attachment is also called Limerence. Limerence differs from sexual infidelity as it is deeply relational and deeply companionate.

The third type of infidelity is the combination of both. More often emotional infidelity, in the long run, leads to sexual infidelity and when such relationships become strong, they are often very difficult to deal with. This infidelity is the strongest type of infidelity because it combines all three biological drives for sex, romance and companionship. Many times, such a relationship among two married people not only affects the partners but also their families. It can be very difficult to end these relations or to move past them.

According to Holmes, other types of affairs fit into combinations of these types like open marriages, swinging, going to sex clubs, having loud affairs, wife-swapping; and the lesser-known or acknowledged infidelity of pornography. Pornography might not seem as infidelity as it is not real, but many people are affected by either themselves having watched pornography or their spouse watching pornography. Many people feel hurt when their partner watches porn and the pain can be as much as real-life infidelity.

So, what type of infidelity are you dealing with?

It is interesting to note that what one person considers as infidelity may not seem like infidelity to someone else. For example, one person may think holding hands isn't cheating because it's not kissing or having sex, and some may not think that looking at porn is a form of cheating since it isn't real. Some people may think that having an inappropriate emotional relationship isn't an affair because there's nothing physical. They're just good friends, so maybe the question behind the question here has more to do with this:

"Do you feel like your trust has been breached? Do you feel like your partner has crossed the line and is it hurting your marriage?"

In situations of doubt, it is worth confirming your doubts by seeking help from friends, family, or even a professional detective. We don't want to dig the entire mountain to realize that it was just a mice! If you are in doubt, keep your fingers crossed and I will pray that maybe it was just your presumption of infidelity and, there is nothing serious to worry about in reality.

And even if it is not your presumption and you are facing a cheating partner, then also don't worry. Just read along with the subsequent chapters, where I reveal how you can deal with these situations.

3 Dealing with Infidelity

Let me begin with an attempt to bring a brief smile on your face. I know that you have a beautiful smile that has been forced to hide amid the crisis. But let me attempt to bring it back with some humour.

A woman was cleaning her husband's dresser drawers when she found 3 golf balls and a box with $2000 in it. She waited for him to come home from the golf course to ask him why these things were hidden in his dresser drawer.

The husband said I'm sorry I hid this from you, but the truth is every time I cheated on you over the last 30 years, I put a golf ball in the drawer.

The wife was very upset at first but after thinking about it said, "I guess 3 times in 30 years is really not that bad! Oh, by the way what is the $2000 in the drawer.

I know that it's a poor joke, but all I am trying is to make you smile first. I am trying to make you realise that whatever you are facing has been faced by several men and women. You are not alone in this world, in this situation. However harsh it may sound, but infidelity has existed and will continue to exist in our society. Truth is often too hard to digest, and that's why the affected partner finds it too harsh to accept what is happening in their life. But the thing is that life is full of surprises, sometimes happy and sometimes sad. Each one of us has difficulties in our lives, and this is bound to happen.

A young child died because of a disease. His mother could not believe that her beloved son was no more. She wept and cried impatiently. Not ready to accept the reality, she approached a famous saint and asked him to bring her son back to life. The saint was having astonishing powers and so he smiled and said, "I will bring your son back to life. The procedure is very simple. I need to chant mantras and throw some water on his body, and he will be alive. But the only condition is that you must bring the water from someone's house who didn't have any death in their family in the past." On hearing this, the lady went to the village in search of water. She knocked on each door in the village and asked for water, but all the houses had witnessed the death of some family members in the past. At the end of the day, the lady realised the truth and accepted it.

Likewise, at the end of the day, you need to accept the truth and digest it. I know that it's hard to digest, but believe me, the first step in finding a solution to the problem is accepting that there is a problem. You may ask thousands of questions like:

"Why me?"
"I have given my 100 percent, then why did it happen?"
"I have never cheated on anyone, then how can someone cheat me?" and so on.

But believe me, these are all nonsense questions, and these questions must be avoided. Instead, accept the situation and ask the right question, which is:

"What should I do now so that my life doesn't remain miserable?"

When you ask this question to yourself, you will find a couple of answers, but ultimately it will all boil down to only three options.

1) Option to continue and ignore.
2) Option to quit and move on
3) Option to continue and bounce back

Trust me, at the end of the day, there are ultimately only three options. Whichever option you choose, you must develop a correct mindset for it and change your thought process to deal with this situation. I highly recommend that you please read the chapter on Developing your Mindset before you finalise on any of the options.

"In life, you have three options with any situation that is a challenge. Remove yourself from the situation, change it or accept it"

Phil Mcgraw

Before we jump into which option is best for you, let us first make you capable of choosing the right option. Capable in the sense that you must not make any decision of your life when you are furious or very sad. When you are angry or in a state of grief, you cannot make the correct decision for your life. And most probably we discuss a decision which is going to affect not only your future but also of your partner and family. So, these decisions are best taken when you are in a calm state of mind.

"I had health insurance for my entire body. But when I claimed my broken heart, it was rejected!"

It is important to see infidelity has existed since marriage was invented. However, it is an irony that we don't consider the broken heart as an illness, though it is more painful than many physical injuries. Dr Kevin Skinner (Clinical Director and Co-Founder of Addo Recovery) in his research found that 7 out of 10 suffering from infidelity are suffering from pain, which is identical to Post Traumatic Stress Disorder (PTSD). These people begin thinking that there is something wrong with them, maybe something is missing in their love and start losing self-confidence. Dr Kevin estimates that six out of ten people have had suicidal thoughts after their spouse's sexual infidelity. So, if you are suffering from infidelity, then you may experience very high levels of stress and anxiety. There is a lot of burden on the heart and soul. So, what to do when you are in such a situation?

There are two aspects of dealing with this situation. First is the external aspect. Believe it or not, a simple stress relieving phenomenon is **communication**. Talk to someone who you think is very close to you. Talk about your stress to your parents or siblings or close friends. A small hug from your parents can relieve stress by a thousand times. Many times, the problem is that the person suffering from such a PTSD does not trust anyone and so refrains from talking about it. But many times things get solved by talking to the right person. Just peep inside you and see if you can find someone with whom you can share this situation, someone who will not only understand you but will also maintain the confidentially of this issue. I have felt that a small chat with your close friends is all it takes to relieve your stress. But what if you don't trust anyone or can't talk to someone about it? Don't worry, focus on the second aspect.

The second aspect is how you communicate with yourself. You need to dive deep inside yourself and gather strength and courage to battle against the situation you are in. Before you decide, you need to be in a calm state of mind. So, for the time-being, before we begin let us first heal the wounded heart. Many ways can help in decreasing the anxiety and pain of the heart. But the method I want to talk about is **Meditate!**

Yes, you read it right, meditate! You must be thinking I am crazy. There is so much pain inside the heart, and how the hell am I supposed to meditate? Well, trust me in whatever condition you are suffering from, it is still ok to meditate just for 10 minutes. 10 minutes a day is a good starting point. Just give yourself 10 minutes and see the magic.

You might think that you can't meditate with a disturbed heart and it is best to meditate when we are in the peace of mind. We should not meditate when we are heavy at heart. Right? Wrong.

Once there was a renowned spiritual leader who was preaching to his disciples. He said, "My dear fellows, whenever you enter the premises of this ashram you must leave behind all your stress and worries outside the ashram and only then you must enter this ashram." Though it sounded perfectly correct, yet it was illogical. One of his disciples got up and asked him, "But Guruji, how do we leave our stress and worries behind? We don't know how to remove stress from our lives, and that is why we visit this ashram. If we already knew how to deal with stress and worries, then what would be the need to visit this ashram."

Exactly true. People visit temples, mosques or churches to remove their worries and connect with GOD. The ones who are having no worries are already in a state of bliss. Similarly, you don't meditate because you are stress-free; you meditate to become stress-free.

Take up the challenge:

Try to meditate just for 10 minutes a day for just 7 days. That is just one hour and 10 minutes of your life that I am asking for. Just meditate 10 minutes every day for 7 days and trust me, you will see the difference. You will find a better person inside you. Remember,

---

"Our bodies heal on their own, But our soul needs our permission to heal".

So first and foremost, permit yourself to heal from these internal wounds that you are suffering from. There may not be an immediate solution visible to you, but in the long term, there is a solution to your problems. So, before you read further just visit any of the links given below and meditate for 10 minutes. I am not asking you from any religious point of view; all I am asking is to meditate either with music or with a mantra or just simply in silence.

Stop reading further and visit any of the links given here based on your preference.

1) Guided Meditation for Healing Broken Hearts (Removing Negative Attachments)

https://www.youtube.com/watch?v=Fj_q6sviH4g

2) A Powerful 10 Minute Guided Meditation

https://www.youtube.com/watch?v=sJH6_ZbgeWQ

3) 10 Minute Guided Meditation to ease Anxiety Worry, Overthinking & Urgency | Soothing Calm | POWERFUL

https://www.youtube.com/watch?v=xoYnqvadurg

4) 1 HOUR of The Best Relaxing Music | Bamboo Flute | - Meditation - Healing - Sleep - Zen - Peace

https://www.youtube.com/watch?v=6ixhN9umyp4

5) 9 HOURS Tibetan Healing Sounds - Singing Bowls - Natural sounds Gold for Meditation & Relaxation

https://www.youtube.com/watch?v=OW7TH2U4hps

6) Infidelity and Cheating Aid

https://www.youtube.com/watch?v=_9unnuZDV5o

7) Turn Cheated into CHANGED. Hypnosis for CHANGE. Just listen.

https://www.youtube.com/watch?v=1xaEFYXcFUQ

Okay, so now honestly answer to yourself: Did you feel a little better now?

With that optimism, let us now proceed further towards dealing with infidelity.

"The thing about meditation is:

You become more and more you."

-David Lynch

---

4 Option to Continue & Ignore

Once again, let me start by attempting to bring a lovely smile on your face. Here is some humour to aid you in smiling.

The old man had 8 hair left on his head. He went to the barbershop.
The barber asked in anger, "Shall I cut or count?"
The old man smiled and said, "Colour it!"

I hope it brings the lovely smile back on your face. Life is to enjoy with whatever you have. And the option of continuing and ignoring the situation is based on this logic. It might seem that this is not an option at all. What is the sense to continue in such a relationship and suffer? But the fact is that many times people don't have choices. When both options are equally bad, people choose the option which is having lesser pain. To understand what I am referring to, let me narrate a true story.

Bhavana (name changed) was married to Himanshu (name changed). Bhavana was born and brought up in a conservative lower-middle-class family. She has two brothers and two sisters. Her father used to work in a textile factory. It was an arranged marriage for Bhavana. In India, except for the big cities, arranged marriages are still very popular. To save money, Bhavana and her younger brother were married on the same day at the same venue, and Bhavana had to wait for almost a year after her engagement. Those days were exquisite for Bhavana. The couple used to meet in the park and often go to watch the movie in the matinee show. The first few years of marriage were pretty romantic for the couple. They lived in a 1 room and kitchen apartment along with Himanshu's widow mother.

But as time passed, Bhavana added some fat and was now a mother of two children. On the other hand, Himanshu would often struggle to meet the expenses, as he earned very little from his job as a peon. As he failed to meet the financial challenges, he started resorting to alcohol to relieve his tensions. After seven years of marriage, the romance among the couple was almost gone except for a few Sundays when the children were out with their grandmother and the couple found some time for each other.

One day Bhavana discovered a packet containing a used condom in Himanshu's pocket. That night when Himanshu returned drunk, she asked Himanshu about it. Himanshu was drunk and had no control over him. He agreed he was visiting a sex worker to meet his sexual urges. When confronted further, he admitted he found

Bhavana to be fat and unromantic. Bhavana was shattered that night. She had little education, but it was easy to realise that she was suffering from sexual infidelity. That night she kept weeping the entire night. The next morning, she again had a conversation with Himanshu, who now refused to admit that he was cheating her. When she showed him the packet of condom, Himanshu had no obvious answer and so just piled up his anger on her and left the house for work. Bhavana knew Himanshu had no intention of changing. She called her mother on the phone and explained to her about the entire situation. But to her surprise, her mother scolded her for becoming fat and ugly and asked her to please and look after Himanshu. Bhavana quickly realised that her mother wanted to help her but was helpless. After the death of her father, her mother could not financially support Bhavana. Her brother earned little to manage his two children and his widow mother and Bhavana and her children would be an additional burden, which they could not afford. Disappointed from her parent's side, Bhavana asked her mother-in-law for help, which did not come. Indian mothers are way too supportive for their sons rather than daughters-in-law. She too bluntly asked her to continue.

Seeing no hope from anywhere, Bhavana slowly started drifting into depression. As days passed her relation with Himanshu worsened. He was now frequently spending his money on sex workers. One night, the couple had a terrible fight. The next morning Bhavana decided enough was enough and having no other options, she decided to commit suicide. It was a Sunday afternoon and everyone was out of the house, so she tried to hang herself from a ceiling fan. But to her luck, her neighbour, Vimlaben, happened to visit her house at that time to borrow sugar. She saw Bhavana trying to hang herself from the window and quickly bumped into the door and rescued Bhavana. Bhavana was in tears as she told her pain to Vimlaben.

Vimlaben was in her forties, and she took Bhavana to her house to counsel her. Vimlaben said, "Are you out of your mind? Have you thought what will happen to your children after you die?"

Bhavana kept crying and muttered, "You will not realize the pain I am going through this moment. You have not faced betrayal in your life".

Vimlaben had tears in her eyes and with full sympathy, she said, "I fully understand your pain, my dear. Ten years ago, I too had discovered that my husband was cheating on me".

Bhavana was shocked and inquired, "How did you deal with the situation then?"

Vimlaben smiled and said, "I did all that I could, I cried, I pleaded, I complained, I even fought but nothing helped. In the end, I had to choose between life and giving up, just like you. And I choose to live not for my husband, not for me, not for my parents, but for my two little children, who were innocent and would have been left stranded had I left them".

Bhavana was full of shame and said, "I am sorry for what I said. Please forgive me."

As both ladies hugged each other, Vimlaben gave a piece of very useful advice to Bhavana, "Listen, dear, it is how you think. Those days I was very disturbed because my husband was enjoying it with other women. But then one day I realised things are not as bad as they seemed. My husband was still coming back home every night, he was still loving his children and trying to manage the family. He was still working and trying to provide us with food and shelter.

So, I changed my thought process and one day I told him that he is free to go to any lady he wants as long as he fed me and my children. I started giving up the daily quarrel because I knew it was of no use. He would not give up, so I gave up and found happiness in all little things. I would often say, he is not bringing step wife. So what if he finds happiness outside? Let him be happy outside, but when he is inside our home, at least I don't want things to be messy. It has been over 10 years now, and he is in his forties and his urges have also subsided now. Happiness comes in bits and pieces, but the problem is that we want it on bigger scales which does not happen most of the time."

Bhavana's attitude towards life changed after that communication. Now she remains happy with her children and ignores her husband's mistakes. "As long as he takes care of me and my children, I don't care what he does outside", she says.

I will not say what Bhavana did is right or wrong. On a personal note, I don't support this option at all. But the thing to note here is that people make their own choices, and we cannot judge people, because to judge people we need to put ourselves into their shoes. What may seem correct to one person will be illogical to others. But we must respect people's choices. I believe many times people make enormous sacrifices for their children and families and we don't have any right to question their decisions. The point to note here is that if you are suffering from infidelity, this option to continue is still one option that many people make depending on their situations.

If you realize I have named this option "Continue and Ignore" and NOT "Continue and Suffer". Often with time things heal up and people don't always suffer. They just ignore and find ways and means to seek happiness, even after continuing the relationship. Having said that, I would strongly recommend that you please evaluate all other options before settling down to any one option.

"Weak people Revenge,

Strong people Forgive,

Intelligent people Ignore".

- Albert Einstein

---

5 Option to quit and move on

In continuation of my efforts to make you smile, here is a little humour to bring back your beautiful smile.

One day it was very crowded in heaven. So, St. Peter started inquiring everyone, "Tell me about the day you died."

The first man said, "Oh, it was awful. I was sure my wife was having an affair, so I came home early to catch her with him. I searched all over the apartment but couldn't find him anywhere. So, I went out onto the balcony, we live on the 25th floor, and found this man hanging over the edge by his fingertips. I went inside, got a hammer, and started hitting his hands. He fell but landed in some bushes. So, I got the refrigerator and pushed it over the balcony, and it crushed him. The strain of the act gave me a heart attack, and I died."

St. Peter couldn't deny that this was a pretty bad day, and since it was a crime of passion, he let the man in.

He then asked the next man in line about the day he died. "Well, sir, it was awful," said the second man. "I was doing aerobics on the balcony of my 26th-floor apartment when I twisted my ankle and slipped over the edge. I grabbed the balcony of the apartment below, but some maniac came out and started pounding on my fingers with a hammer. Luckily, I landed in some bushes, but then the guy dropped a refrigerator on me!"

St. Peter chuckled, let him into heaven and moved further.

"Tell me about the day you died?", he said to the third man in line.

"OK, picture this, I'm naked, hiding inside a refrigerator ... "

Hope that it brings some relief and makes you feel comfortable. So now, coming to the option of quitting; even before you consider this option, please make sure you have exhausted all other options. Another important thing to note is,

---

**"Don't take Divorce decision in a moment,
Compile moments from several months to
decide on divorce"**

Taking a divorce is the last but not the least option, which one should resort to. Exhaust all your resources and plans before you succumb to ending your relationship. Never decide in any hurry. Ending a relationship is going to be painful, especially if you have loved your partner at some point in time. But then, just because you love someone does not mean that your love should be taken for granted. I will not address the legalities of divorce, because I am not the best person to do so. But I would like to touch upon other important aspects. Deciding when to quit is very essential, there is a clear line between sacrificing and being fooled. Let me again start with a real-life example.

Reema (name changed) was born and brought up in a rich family. She was beautiful, smart and intelligent. She was studying sociology at a well-known University. Rajesh (name changed) was studying Law at the same university. Both met each other during the annual cultural festival. They both were competing for annual college drama representing their respective colleges. Initially, it started with rivalry, but as happens in films, their rivalry slowly turned out into friendship, and later love. As their love progressed, both went for love marriage. Rajesh was coming from a middle-class family, and so Reema's parents initially had a strong opposition to this relationship. However, because of the couple's sustained efforts, both ended up in marriage after convincing families. The initial days of married life were super exciting for the couple, but after a few years went by, Rajesh got occupied in his court matters and could hardly get time for Reema.

Reema was fed up living a middle-class life in Rajesh's family. She was used to having servants serving her at her parent's house and here she had to work on her own. She would long for romantic getaways with Rajesh, which decreased with time. She was emotionally and financially unsatisfied in her relationship.

Soon, she started dating her old childhood friend Vicky, who always had a crush on her. Vicky was a rich businessperson and would take Reema to parties and discotheque, giving Reema the life she always wanted to live in. It was not long before Rajesh came to know about their relationship. Rajesh loved Reema very much. He wanted to give her all the luxuries in life. So, he used to work hard to earn more, but in earning, he was sacrificing his time with Reema. Rajesh realised Reema wanted to live a rich life and no matter how hard he was trying; she was not recognising his efforts. Rajesh tried to communicate with Reema; he asked her for a few years so he could make up from the middle class to the rich class, but Reema kept on asking for immediate attention. According to Reema, there was no point in enjoying life after years have gone by. The couple loved each other, but their financial status and ideologies were taking a toll on their relationship. Their relationship tanked day by day and it was not until finally, the couple called it a quit.

Life can be hard. Couples have different priorities in life, and it is very necessary that at some point in time these priorities converge. Reema wanted to live her life king-size because she was used to living a posh life. Rajesh was conservative in his approach, as he had seen his family struggle financially all his life. This difference in ideologies was difficult to converge, and so after giving enough time for brainstorming, the couple filed a divorce. If you see the situation from a third perspective, both Reema and Rajesh were correct from their point of view. Reema had seen how her friend circle was enjoying their life and she found herself stuck in the role of a middle-class homemaker which she never wanted to become. Rajesh wanted a conservative homemaker with a simple lifestyle. Unfortunately, it was a clash of ideologies and so it was justified for the couple to end their relationship. Let me discuss another real-life example.

Veena (name changed) was married to Vinay (name changed). It was an arranged marriage. Earlier Veena had an engagement with Prakash (name changed) but that did not last long. A month before their marriage, their relationship was called off by the families. Veena was already in her thirties and for her, marrying after a broken engagement was like a miracle. In conservative Indian families, even today, it is very hard to find a match for a girl who has had a broken engagement. So, Veena was very cautious in her approach, and she wanted to make sure that her marriage goes off well. But on the first night of the marriage itself, Vinay struggled to make physical love to Veena. Veena was very caring and understanding.

"It's okay, dear. It happens", she said to Vinay.

But as days passed by, Vinay could not get proper erections. "It takes time. My friend took almost a year to have proper physical relations" explained Vinay. Veena was a shy Indian girl, and so she quietly accepted the situation. Even when the couple went for their honeymoon almost after three months to the Philippines, Vinay struggled to get proper erections. Vinay would often now avoid attempting physical intimacy and would claim to be tired and out of the mood. Poor Veena thought it might take time for men to make love. She continued her relationship with full faith and devotion. She was an excellent housewife who would take full care of Vinay's parents. Days turned into months and months now into a year. Veena's parents started questioning Veena about having a baby. Veena skilfully ignored these questions. Vinay now started refraining from making physical contact.

One day after almost one and half years of marriage, Veena asked Vinay to consult a doctor and discuss the issue, but Vinay bluntly rejected saying,

"It's you who is having a problem. You turn me off and so I don't get erections. It's your fault, so if you better get yourself checked. I am perfectly normal."

Man's ego was preventing Vinay from accepting that it was his fault. Veena truly loved Vinay and did not want to disappoint him. So, one day poor Veena went to see a Gynaecologist under the excuse of urine infection. The lady doctor examined her and found her completely normal. So, it was now clear to Veena it was Vinay who was having a fault running away from her. Veena did not want to expose Vinay, and so she kept mum. But then other issues started building up then. Vinay's mother started mentally torturing her. Minor issues started leading to big quarrels.

One day after two years of marriage, Vinay called Veena's parents to complain about Veena. Initially, Veena's parents listened carefully to all complaints about Veena, which were all minor. But it did not stop there. It went on and on and on. After almost one and a half hours of discussion, finally, Veena broke into tears and told her parents about Vinay's problem.

Veena's parents were in a shock. Veena's father lost his temper and scolded Vinay badly for hiding this issue for two years. They then took Veena to their place. Veena kept weeping for several days; she wanted to go back to Vinay. She loved him and was even ready to live life with him, even if he could not satisfy her physically for her entire life. Veena waited for several days, expecting Vinay to come and take her back. Vinay would not receive her phone and would not reply to her messages; he claimed he was very upset with how Veena's father had bullied him. Veena's brother went to meet Vinay and apologise for the issue. But nothing happened. After two-and-a-half months, Vinay sent a legal notice to Veena, stating that Veena was not coming back to him, and her parents were stopping her from returning to him. It was now clear to Veena's parents that it was time to call off the relationship, but Veena did not want to stay with her parents. She kept crying every day and wanted to go back to Vinay, but after some days a divorce case was filed in the court. Veena knew now nobody would accept her, as she had one broken engagement and one divorce to her name, but her parents were very supportive, and they convinced her it was a dead-end and she had to end her relationship. Veena then agreed to file a divorce case after waiting for almost six months at her parent's place.

With Veena, as it might be apparent from an outsider perspective, it makes no sense to continue the relationship despite her genuine love for Vinay. But if you put yourself in the place of Veena, it is a terrible situation. She can't depart from the one she loves and is even ready to live with him even if they don't have kids for her entire life. In time, she even thought that she would adopt children, if required. But the point here is if their relationship had continued peacefully, maybe her approach was correct.

It is very difficult to find genuine love and if you find genuine love; you are ready to let go of a lot of things for your love. It is very difficult to judge people because we don't know how their bonding with their partners is. But one thing is sure, if there is love, then it should be both ways. Here, despite the quarrel, Vinay should have come back to take Veena home. But he went on another path, leaving no choice for Veena. Many times, I have seen that when there is a very strong emotional infidelity, the cheating partner wants to get rid of his existing marriage and start a new beginning with the new partner. In such cases, no matter how strongly the person loves his partner, eventually, things can ultimately fall on the path of divorce. When things are so bad, one needs to come out of the love barrier and think with a broader perspective.

"Divorce is like a Chemotherapy and must not be taken otherwise. But when the relationship is as bad as cancer, it is the only choice to survive."

Jiten Bhatt

It also reminds me of a famous quote by American writer, Jennifer Weiner. She says,

---

"Divorce isn't such a tragedy. A tragedy's staying in an unhappy marriage, teaching your children the wrong things about love. Nobody ever died of divorce".

- Jennifer Weiner

---

6 Option to Continue & bounce back

As usual, let me begin this chapter by trying to bring back some lovely smile on your face.

Husband, "When I get mad at you, you never fight back. How do you control your anger?"
Wife, "I clean the toilet."
Husband, "How does that help?"
Wife, "I use your toothbrush!!"

I hope it brings the lovely smile back on your face. Coming to this last option, this is the option that I love and recommend to all as the first option to try. And believe me, this is the hardest of all other options because it calls for a lot of effort from both partners. Once again let me start with an example, which was quoted by the English writer, broadcaster, psychotherapist and TEDx speaker, Lucy Beresford.

Lucy had a client named Hattie (name changed). She had a high-flying career, three healthy kids and eighteen years of marriage. She had everything in her life, a caring husband, Will (name changed), who was a musician. Hattie had always been the golden child, much loved by her family, never flunked an exam and never taken drugs, whereas Will had an unconventional upbringing. He was sent in and out of various boarding schools and emotionally detached from his parents.

He was drawn to Hattie for her stability and her focus. Hattie was drawn to will for his slightly more creative, laid-back style. Both of them had spent an excellent time as a couple. But one day Will opened Hattie's phone for checking details of a family holiday flight, and was shocked to see those texts from Hattie's colleague, Stuart. The texts clarified his wife had been having an affair since two years. Suddenly, this fantastic couple was in a crisis; Will was heartbroken and furious. Hattie had no explanations and was deeply ashamed. Will had a tough time and the one thought that kept circling in his mind was,

"Should I stay, or should I quit?"

Hattie could only see a broken, furious man in Will. Will could only see a monstrous woman who'd broken his heart and ruptured his family. It was a really hard time for the couple. But if you are in such a moment, you must realise that if a partner is repenting for what he or she has done, then it's equally important for you to forgive and forget to move ahead in life.

Lucy says that from her 20 years of experience as a psychotherapist and radio agony aunt, she is convinced that though other options may sound good, the more courageous option is to stay and rebuild that relationship.

"The couples that are 'meant to be' are the ones who go through everything that is meant to tear them apart and come out even stronger than they were before." - Anonymous

---

There are many examples of couples who have survived such a situation. Take for example Hollywood celebrity couple rapper Jay-Z and singer Beyonce. When Jay-Z cheated on his wife, in an interview with the New York Times he said that "When you see on the face of your beloved, the pain caused by your cheating it makes you want to run away, hide, quit the relationship and never come back". Jay-Z and his wife, Beyonce, looked inwards. They faced their pain and emerged to rebuild a reinvigorated relationship with each other and writing a couple of albums in the process.

Rebuilding a relationship is not as easy as it calls for both partners to work out a path towards getting back together. Lucy calls it an SOS situation. It is a crisis time for the couple. The betrayer needs to take ownership of what he or she has done and must apologise sincerely. Just a sorry will not work here. A lot more effort is required to repair and regain the trust that has been lost among partners, and it is not only difficult but also time-consuming.

The one who is betrayed also has a lot to do. He or she can't just blame it all on the other partner. According to Lucy, if your partner was 99% responsible for the mess you are currently going through, then it still leaves 1% for you to look at and own and work on it. The very thing that will bring you together and will keep you together as a couple will be the thing that threatens to blow it.

According to Dr Nisha Khanna, who is a psychologist, most of the time almost 90 to 95 percent of the time, the cheating partners are emotionally unstable. They are emotionally unstable. So, with Hattie, she found Will was always busy with his music and was not giving enough attention and love to her. Though Will may not realize it, somewhere down the line, he too has been missing to hit the targets, which disappointed Hattie and forced her to look for someone outside her marriage.

We all are emotional beings. From my experience in my life, I can tell that each person no matter how strong he/she appears has an emotionally weak zone where he or she needs love and care. Especially in today's scenario, when life is fast and we talk less in one to one and text more through phones, each couple is vulnerable to some extent. So, in these times of distress, one must practise forgiveness and acceptance. Believe me, if you are to choose this option (and I would recommend you choose this option), you will need a lot of patience and an enormous heart. I am NOT saying you have to stay forever in a breached relationship, but please give it some time and look within and you may very well fall back in love with your partner.

Quitting a relationship in a hurry is foolish. You will anyway be in a win-win situation if you continue. Either you will see your partner with fresh eyes, new passion, and new compassion, or you learn about yourself to move forward with confidence into the next healthier relationship. Many times, when the divorced couples meet after several years, they realise that even after several years their bonding is still very strong, and it would have been much better if they had given each other a second chance. If your relationship is broken, at least you know you were open not just to repairing it, but to growing as a person instead of splitting apart. Give some time to your relationship to heal. Time is the biggest healer, and it will be okay as days pass by.

"Never leave a genuine relationship for a few faults. Nobody is perfect, nobody is correct, and in the end, affection is always greater than perfection." - Anonymous

---

Eventually, in the journey to continuing your relationship, you will at some point in time have to practise forgiveness. It's really hard to forgive someone and continue to love when they have cheated on you. But believe me, it is also a way of life and becoming a better person yourself.

"Forgiveness is for you - not the other person. It's something you do inside yourself, that you feel in your body and heart, that releases you from your past and frees you to live life fully."

- Barbara J. Hunt

When you practise forgiveness, you are not only helping your partner to recover your relationship but are yourself helping to heal your wounds. You will feel a much different person when you forgive and let go of things.

After forgiving, your heart will feel much lighter, and you will rejuvenate with inner happiness. Compassion and Forgiveness are the two greatest qualities that a humans practise in their life.

Let me support my argument with another real-life example. Kelsey Grant is an author and relationship coach. In her life, she has faced several instances of infidelity. and every time she has come back strong and regained her relationship. Her relationship began when she met her husband unexpectedly at Gay Pride. It was an outstanding experience and she fell in love with him. After her marriage, she loved her husband very much, and this love resulted in the feeling of insecurity. She became more insecure and as time passed by, her fears turned into reality. Eventually, she learned from those instances and transformed herself into a much stronger human being. She decided she will transform herself by diving deeper into what was causing her lack of self-confidence. What she discovered was that it was a lack of self-love that had been causing her to lose her self-confidence. For the next five months, she dived into the world of self-love, exploring all resources that she could get. She overcame all her fears and eventually regained back the control of her life. But her patience and loyalty were tested once again after several years when she came across some texts on her husband's phone. Had she been the old, scared wife, she would have turned into a rage monster and lost her temper. But having done a lot of work on herself in the last two years, she kept calm and did something different this time. Even though she was feeling furious, betrayed and upset, she could sit there with an open heart and discuss things with her partner. She practised compassion and did something which was not expected from her. She reached out to the other woman and wrote her a message,

"Hey, I just found your communication with my partner and it's not okay. It needs to stop and woman-to-woman I don't get that this is the impact that you want to leave the world with. I have a deep sense that you're in pain you know like your relationship with him has been in the shadows that's painful enough, but I also get the sense that you probably wanted something more from him than he was ever willing or capable of giving you. That's no excuse for you to go out and hurt someone else."

Within moments of sending that message, the other lady wrote back, "I am sorry for having caused you so much pain. I don't know how you can be so kind to me after what I've done to you." Kelsey replied, "Because that's what you deserve. You deserve compassion. You deserve respect. You deserve the honour. You deserve forgiveness. You deserve unconditional love and if I can extend that to you there's no reason why you can't find that for yourself inside and if you learn how to give yourself unconditional love forgiveness and acceptance, you will set yourself on a new course in life in love."

I have seen several women take it to a dog fight when they discover another woman is ruining their married life. But what Kelsey did was different; not only did it compel the other lady to realise her mistakes, but she also turned a beautiful woman to woman relationship. Even Mahatma Gandhi has said,

**"Forgiveness is choosing to love. It is the first skill of self-giving love.
The weak can never forgive.
Forgiveness is the attribute of the strong."
- Mahatma Gandhi**

Eventually all couples in the world face a time of crisis at some point or other. Only the crisis can be of different forms. For some of them, this crisis is Infidelity, for some it is a lack of communication, for some it is declining sexual intimacy, for some it is waning appreciation, and for others it is progressive quarrels. Whatever be the crisis, you must realize that each relationship is tested at some time or other. And it is not these hard times that define the relationship, but it is how you deal in such times that do.

"It's not the rough times endured that define your relationship, it is how you deal with them and how you bounce back".
– Mark W. Boyer

So, when you face an infidelity crisis, sit down and think about how you can get your train back on the track. Spend some time with your inner self. Practise meditation, practice forgiveness. It is not for your past, but it is for your future.

"Forgiveness is a powerful thing.
It doesn't change what has happened;
it changes what is to come."
-   Janeen Latini

So, will your relationship survive if you forget and move ahead? Or will your partner cheat you again? Well, honestly, these answers are hard to predict. But at least when you put the effort in the right direction, it will lead to fruitful results. So, I leave it to you to decide what you want to focus your attention on.

"At the end of the day, you can either focus on what's tearing you apart or
what's holding you together".
- Anonymous

7 Developing your Mindset

Let me start this chapter by sharing a famous joke shared by Sadhguru Jaggi Vasudev.

A man met his close college friend after twenty-five years. So, he invited him for dinner at his place. His wife was serving them traditional Indian food. Every time the man wanted something, he would call out his wife with beautiful words such as,

"Honey, can you pass me the curd",

"Sweetheart, can you bring me the chapatti",

"Darling, can you please bring me some rice",

"My sweetie, please bring dal to us",

"My bulbul we have finished eating please take back the plates" and so on.

After dinner was done, at the time of leaving, his friend said,

"My dear friend, you have a lovely life. I have been married for fifteen years now and I and my wife don't even look at each other's face. And the way you are bonding with your wife is truly fantastic."

The man said, "What are you talking about? I did not get it."

His friend said, "You called her Sweetheart, you called her bulbul, you called her sweetie."

The man said to his friend, "No man, it's not like that. I forgot her name seven years ago!"

I hope that adds to your smile today. Before I begin this chapter, I would like to acknowledge that the thoughts expressed in this chapter are taken from Sadhguru's talk, whose link is given in references.

When asked about Infidelity and punishing the betrayer, Sadhguru explains people are doing what they want to do, not what we want them to do. That may not be in our interest, but they're doing what they want to do. He is not commenting on whether it is right or wrong. All he is suggesting is to understand the mechanics of the situation. In his own words, Sadhguru says,

"Somebody is doing what they want to do. They're breaking an understanding between two people. But probably you

misunderstood understanding. You believed these understandings are absolute, but they are not. Nowhere in the history of humanity or today or at any time in the future will human relationships be absolute. Though every person who gets a little romantic believes that his relationship is going to be an absolute relationship, there is no such thing about it. A relationship is always a variable. You have to conduct it daily. One day if you don't conduct it properly, it may go somewhere. You have to conduct it right.

You may say that you are doing your best. But somebody feels your best is not good enough for them. I want you to come to terms with this. I am not saying what they're doing is right or wrong, that is not for me to say. All I am saying is that this is how human beings are functioning for ages.

First, you need to understand that relationships will never be absolute. They will be variables. You are juggling with fireballs. Sometimes it will spill out. It takes a lot of skill and attention to keep juggling in relationships. You need to understand this - a relationship is a variable reality, it is not an absolute reality. If you want to have an absolute relationship, you must hold relationships with the dead. That's the reason why many people choose God, because it's an absolute relationship. You can handle it whichever way you want. If you didn't think of him for ten days and on the 11th day if you think of him, God is still there. You do that with your husband or wife, then something else will happen. You went away, got busy, forgot about God for three years and again you can think of him, God is still there. So, if you want to have an absolute relationship, you should not choose human beings.

Human relationships are variables that need a lot of attention. When your illusions are broken, you are disillusioned. It is a wonderful thing if your illusions are broken because it means life is bringing you closer to reality. So, this is an opportunity for you to sit down and see what the nature of life is. This piece of life is a complete piece of life. It isn't half a life; it is a full life. Then why is it that it feels so incomplete? It needs another person to fill this life. It's time to look at it. If this is a full life, this is complete by itself. But right now, you made it in such a way that this life cannot exist with that one. So somewhere it's an incomplete life, or at least the fullness of life's nature isn't realised. This is a complete piece of life packed with creator and creation together in a very great combination.

When life knocks at your door like this, it's time you look deeper rather than reacting and trying to fix somebody else. Punishing somebody else will not transform your life nor going to make your life beautiful in any way. So don't go that way this is an opportunity somebody is opening up a spiritual dimension for you somebody is making you realise how fragile all these things are. They can cheat you, they can run away, they can divorce you or they can fall dead. If they fall dead, you wouldn't think that your partner cheated you. The important thing is you are denied something; How he did it is not the problem.

He or she denied you something either by death or cheating or whatever you call it, but essentially you got denied. You can be denied only because you are in a certain illusory state of believing that this is half a life, and it needs another half from somewhere. But no, this is a complete life.

If you blossom as a complete life, you will see relationships will be completely different. It will be more of coming together and sharing and not of extracting. This is a great opportunity as somebody has given you a stop and is pushing you towards ultimate reality from an illusory state. We must thank that person for not keeping you in an illusion for an entire lifetime. Otherwise, you will know this at the time of your death.

Yes, you'll know at the time when you're dying. At the time of death, you ask your partner I'm scared why don't you come with me? The answer will be no and so instead of knowing that last moment, it's better to know now".

Indeed! What a great level of thinking! When I heard this, even I was left dazzled. Because Sadhguru added an extra dimension to handling infidelity. While most western psychologists and relationship experts emphasised other aspects of dealing with infidelity Sadhguru stressed on looking deep inside and realising that all relationships are fragile and the entire concept that you are incomplete without your partner is fake. Think about these thoughts for a while.

In my opinion, you can leave out the spirituality part if that does not suit you. But you need to develop your mindset, so you are not affected by routine stresses developing in the relationship. Please realise that:

"The only constant in life is change"

- Heraclitus.

So, no matter how good your partner is or was in the past, change is bound to happen. You can't complain because you also change with time. Everyone changes with time.

"Changed People, Change People"

- Anonymous.

You are not the same person you were two years ago. So, in this ever-changing world, you cannot expect a happy relationship from your partner every time. It is illogical and impractical. Remember the famous Murphy's law.

"Whatever can go wrong, will go wrong"

Edward A Murphy

If that law is true, every relationship can go wrong. This is a frightening situation. So, what to do? Well, don't worry, because the reverse is also true. This is what I call reverse Murphy's law for healing.

"Whatever can be healed, will eventually get healed" - Jiten Bhatt

---

So, at the end of the day, relationships will be okay, and your wounded heart will heal. Time is the biggest healer. But the real question that is of importance is how fast can we heal? The answer to this hard question is,

---

"You can't heal your heart as long as you want to. But the good news is, you can heal your heart as fast as you want to." - Jiten Bhatt

---

So don't worry, you can heal as fast as you allow your heart to heal. When you focus on problems in your relationship, you will stop your heart from healing. I am not saying that problems will go away fast. Problems will remain, but you will be a much happier person when you change your attitude.

And before we jump to conclusions, a word of caution, which I want to highlight. This is taken from the book "Everything is f*cked" by "Mark Manson"; one of the paradoxes pointed out in this book is about the relationship. A boy and girl are in a relationship and the boy cheats the girl. The girl is left heartbroken. Her experience leaves her with two options. Option A is to think that all men are shit and Option B is that it's her fault and she is shit. Since both options are equally bad, she chooses option A and builds an opinion that all men are shit. A few years later, a decent man comes into her life. But she has gone with option A, she just dumps him because she thinks all men are shit. This man is now heartbroken and so again he has now two options to make an opinion. Option A: All women are shit and Option B: He is shit. So again, he goes for Option A, and this leads to a chain reaction. He now goes and cheats another decent girl because he has gone for option A. So, you need to understand that before building any generalized opinion please look into a practical aspect. Just because your partner has cheated you, does not mean that all men or women will cheat. Please be open to accept this and move forward in your life.

"Beware of half-truths, You may have gotten hold of wrong half". - Anonymous.

---

8 Concluding Remarks

"A conclusion is the place where you get tired of thinking". Arthur Bloch

As has been my attempt, let me start the final concluding remarks with some humour for you.

A woman was giving her driving license test at RTO. The officer asked her,
"If you are driving fast and suddenly see your husband and brother walking in your way. What will you hit first?"
Lady said, "I will hit my husband!"
Officer said, "Mam, this is 3rd time I am telling you, hit the brake first!!"

Hope that it brings some smile on your face. Let me try again.

A woman was giving her driving license test at RTO. The officer asked her,
"If you are driving fast and suddenly see your husband and brother walking in your way. What will you hit first?"
Lady said, "I will hit my husband!"

Officer said, "Mam, this is 3rd time I am telling you, hit the brake first!!"

Hope that it brings some smile again on your face. Let me try again.

A woman was giving her driving license test at RTO. The officer asked her,
"If you are driving fast and suddenly see your husband and brother walking in your way. What will you hit first?"
Lady said, "I will hit my husband!"
Officer said, "Mam, this is 3rd time I am telling you, hit the brake first!!"

Hope that it brings some smile on your face. Let me give one more try.

A woman was giving her driving license test at RTO. The officer asked her,
"If you are driving fast and suddenly see your husband and brother walking in your way. What will you hit first?"
Lady said, "I will hit my husband!"
Officer said, "Mam, this is 3rd time I am telling you, hit the brake first!!"

No, it's not a typo error. Did you laugh at the same joke again and again? I know you didn't. That brings us to a very important lesson taught by Gaur Gopal Dasji,

Think about it. You have spent so many sleepless hours pondering over the problem of infidelity. You have cried again and again over your cheating partner. Haven't you? But there is no point in focusing again and again on your problems. You need to focus on solutions to problems. You need to grant permission to your heart, so it heals.

It's time to move on and make some decisions about it. You can't keep on crying for your entire life. You don't want to be fighting over the same issue again and again. It's time that you sit down and think about what your options are and how you want to go about them.

People suffer because of their indecisiveness. You can't hang on to multiple options at the same time. You will have to choose one option. By deferring the decision, you are eventually choosing the option to ignore and continue. Please don't stand in the middle of the crossroads. Walk down to either side of the crossroad.

"Time doesn't wait. Indecision will only let opportunities slip by.

Pick a path and walk confidently with your heart behind every step".

Doe Zantamata

I have seen many couples suffer a lot because they want both things in life at the same time. They want to continue because they still love their partners, and they also want things to change.

"If you change nothing, nothing changes".

Joyce Brothers

Based on my experience of life and infidelity, I have put forward all that I think can be done. Hope that it makes some sense. In the end, I would say learn to be happy with whatever decision you take.

It's okay to compromise if that helps save many lives. It's also okay to quit if that saves many lives and makes you happy. And last but not the least, it's also okay to continue and attempt to bounce back. Your attitude will determine how you will go ahead in your life.

So please do yourself a favour. Get up and fight against your problems. It does not matter how you fight and which option you take, what matters is that you take a step further.

I hope this book has helped you in some manner. If you liked the book, it would be very nice of you if you can leave an honest review of this book. Your feedback is precious to me. You can directly reach the review page on Amazon sites using the following links/QR codes:

AMAZON.COM   AMAZON.CO.UK   AMAZON.IN

I research plenty of stuff and then try to bring out the essence of the matter in my articles. My newsletter typically includes articles on self-motivation, time management, business management, way to find happiness in life, and on fighting depression, stress and anxiety. You can have a look at my articles and subscribe to my newsletter by clicking to my website https://jitenhbhatt.com/

If you feel worthy, then you may share your experience of infidelity and whether this book was of any help to you. Just connect with me by dropping a mail to jiten@jitenhbhatt.com. Once again, I thank you for reading my book. May GOD bless you and your family. May you come out of your troubles and be happy always. Let God spread peace and joy everywhere.

"It is important that you learn to smile because life will anyway teach you to cry"

– Jiten Bhatt

---

9 References

- Infidelity: to stay or go...? | Lucy Beresford | TEDxFolkestone

  https://www.youtube.com/watch?v=5TUxH2izTGI

- The Other Side of Infidelity | Dr Kevin Skinner | TEDxRiverton

  https://www.youtube.com/watch?v=NBPmZJEsaAA

- What To Do When Your Loved One Cheats On You??? | Sadhguru About Relationships |

  https://www.youtube.com/watch?v=IHDIRH8T75E

- How to deal with infidelity

  https://www.youtube.com/watch?v=pFV8rtOyGT0

- The gifts of infidelity | Kelsey Grant | TEDxGastownWomen

  https://www.youtube.com/watch?v=ph1HHXEC6RU

- Dealing with infidelity in marriage | Understand Cheating

  https://www.youtube.com/watch?v=UsZ81vMKijQ

About the Author

Jiten is a PhD from Nirma University & M. Tech from IIT Bombay. He is an author & an Ex-ISRO Engineering scientist. He also holds a Diploma in Creative English. He has authored several books and articles. You can connect with him on his blog,

https:\\jitenhbhatt.com

Freebies for you

As a token of gratitude for your purchase, I would like to gift you with wide range of freebies (including e-books, printables and other freebies). Please download one or all of them from the following link.

https://store.jitenhbhatt.com/download-your-free-gifts/

My blog contains several articles on various topics, which might interest you. Please have a look at my website here.

https://jitenhbhatt.com/

Once again, thank you for purchasing this book.

God Bless You and keep smiling.